WE THE PEOPLE

WRITING THE CONSTITUTION

Virginia Loh-Hagan

45TH PARALLEL PRESS

Published in the United States of America by Cherry Lake Publishing
Ann Arbor, Michigan
www.cherrylakepublishing.com

Reading Adviser: Beth Walker Gambro, MS, Ed., Reading Consultant, Yorkville, IL
Cover Designer: Felicia Macheske

Photo Credits: © mizar_21984/Shutterstock.com, cover, 1; © Everett Historical/Shutterstock.com, 5;
© zimmytws/Shutterstock.com, 6; © Andy Vinnikov/Shutterstock.com, 11; © Morocko/Shutterstock.com, 12;
© zstock/Shutterstock.com, 15; © kiwiofmischief/Shutterstock.com, 19; © Rena Schild/Shutterstock.com, 21;
© Steve Heap/Shutterstock.com, 22; © Cavan-Images/Shutterstock.com, 25

Graphic Elements Throughout: © Chipmunk131/Shutterstock.com; © Nowik Sylwia/Shutterstock.com;
© Andrey_Popov/Shutterstock.com; © NadzeyaShanchuk/Shutterstock.com; © KathyGold/Shutterstock.com;
© Black creator/Shutterstock.com; © Edvard Molnar/Shutterstock.com; © Elenadesign/Shutterstock.com;
© estherpoon/Shutterstock.com

45th Parallel Press is an imprint of Cherry Lake Publishing.

Library of Congress Cataloging-in-Publication Data
Names: Loh-Hagan, Virginia, author.
Title: We the people : writing the Constitution / by Virginia Loh-Hagan.
Description: Ann Arbor : Cherry Lake Publishing, [2022] | Series: Behind the curtain
Identifiers: LCCN 2021037485 | ISBN 9781534199507 (hardcover) | ISBN 9781668900642 (paperback) |
    ISBN 9781668902080 (pdf) | ISBN 9781668906408 (ebook)
Subjects: LCSH: United States. Constitution—Juvenile literature. | Suffrage—United States—Juvenile literature. |
    United States—Politics and government—1783-1789—Juvenile literature.
Classification: LCC E303 .L64 2022 | DDC 342.7302/9—dc23
LC record available at https://lccn.loc.gov/2021037485

Cherry Lake Publishing would like to acknowledge the work of the Partnership for 21st Century Learning,
a Network of Battelle for Kids. Please visit *http://www.battelleforkids.org/networks/p21* for more information.

Printed in the United States of America
Corporate Graphics

A Note on Dramatic Retellings

Participating in Readers Theater, or dramatic retellings, can greatly improve reading skills, especially fluency. The books in the **BEHIND THE CURTAIN** series give readers opportunities to learn about important historical events in a fun and engaging way. These books serve as a bridge to more complex texts. All the characters and stories have been fictionalized. To learn more, check out the Perspectives Library series and the Modern Perspectives series, as **BEHIND THE CURTAIN** books are aligned to these stories.

TABLE of CONTENTS

HiSTORiCAL BACKGROUND

The Articles of Confederation were created in 1777. It was the United States's first governing document. It had problems. The national government was weak. States operated like separate countries.

In 1783, the United States won its freedom from Great Britain. A stronger federal government was needed. The United States was unstable. It was open to attacks.

In 1786, Alexander Hamilton called for meetings. He wanted to create a constitution. Many leaders showed up. They created a national government. They included checks and balances. Power was spread between a central government and states. These meetings were held in secret. Reporters were banned. No visitors were allowed.

Vocabulary

confederation
(kuhn-feh-duh-RAY-shuhn)
a union of people or groups

federal (FEH-duh-ruhl) a form of government where power is shared between a central government and states

constitution (kahn-stuh-TOO-shuhn)
the basic principles and laws
of a nation

FLASH FACT!

At first, there were only 10 amendments to the Constitution. As of 2021, there are 27.

People The United States
Article 1

1st Amendment

Vocabulary

amendments (uh-MEHND-muhnts) changes or additions to improve a law or document

Federalists supported the Constitution. Hamilton and James Madison wrote several essays. They wanted people to vote for the new government. These essays were called The Federalist Papers.

Anti-Federalists didn't support the Constitution. They were worried about giving too much power to the government. They wanted to make sure people had rights. They pushed for a Bill of Rights. The Bill of Rights contains the first 10 amendments to the Constitution. They were added in 1791. These amendments guarantee political freedoms. Examples are freedom of speech, religion, and the press.

The U.S. Constitution was signed in 1787. It starts with these words: "We the People of the United States . . . ."

CAST of CHARACTERS

NARRATOR: person who helps tells the story

WILLIAM: a lawyer living in 1787

ROBERT: a worker who prints newspapers living in 1787

MERCY: a female **domestic servant** living in 1787

JESSICA: a young student living in 2022

RANDY: a young student living in 2022

SALLY: a young student living in 2022

SPOTLIGHT
AMPLIFICATION OF AN ACTIVIST

Stacey Abrams is a Black activist. She fights for voting rights. She served in the Georgia House of Representatives. In 2018, she ran for governor of Georgia. She won the Democratic nomination. She became the first Black woman to be a major party's nominee for governor. She lost the election. Some election law experts said the election was unfair. Many voters were denied votes. Abrams started Fair Fight Action. This group fights against voter suppression. It promotes fair elections. It encourages voter participation and provides education. In 2020, Abrams helped win votes for President Biden. She increased Democratic votes. She registered more than 800,000 new voters.

Vocabulary
domestic servant
(duh-MEH-stik SUHR-vuhnt)
someone who performs housework
for a living

FLASH FACT!
The U.S. Constitution is the oldest written national constitution in use.

NARRATOR: *It is 1787. The nation's leaders are in Philadelphia, Pennsylvania.* **WILLIAM** *and* **ROBERT** *are having dinner at William's house.*

WILLIAM: The **convention** has started. Have you heard any news?

ROBERT: I've heard nothing. All the **delegates** have taken **oaths** of silence.

WILLIAM: We should know what's happening. It's our right.

ROBERT: They're trying to keep some order. They don't want to worry about public opinion.

WILLIAM: That makes sense. It sounds like they want to avoid **partisan** politics. But they're going too far.

ROBERT: What do you mean?

WILLIAM: Guards stand outside the meeting hall. They only let in delegates.

Vocabulary

convention (kuhn-VEHN-shuhn) a meeting of people gathered for a common purpose

delegates (DEH-lih-guhts) people chosen to represent others

oaths (OHTHZ) vows or promises

partisan (PAR-tuh-zuhn) strongly supporting one side

FLASH FACT!

Politics today is partisan. It's usually Republicans versus Democrats.

ROBERT: They also throw dirt on the streets. The streets are made of **cobblestone**. Dirt keeps the street noise down. This helps the delegates hear each other better.

WILLIAM: Also, all the windows are closed. They must be really hot.

ROBERT: They must be uncomfortable. They're committed to their oaths.

WILLIAM: I wish we knew more. I want to know what they're talking about.

ROBERT: We can get information from the Federalist Papers.

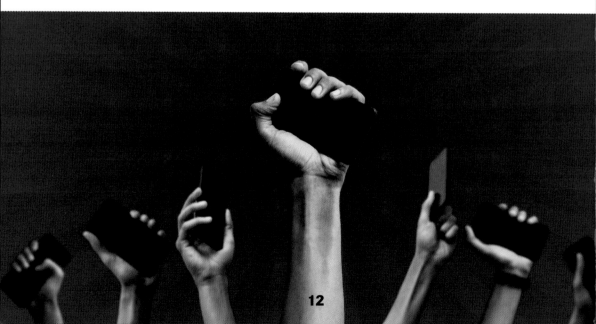

WILLIAM: Do you know who is writing those?

ROBERT: No one really knows. They're all signed from "Publius."

WILLIAM: What does that mean?

ROBERT: It's Latin for "the people." The writers want to be **anonymous**.

WILLIAM: Your newspaper has been publishing the papers. You must have an idea of who wrote them.

Vocabulary

cobblestone (KAH-buhl-stohn) made of small, round stones

anonymous (uh-NAH-nuh-muhss) not named or identified

FLASH FACT!

Today, social media has increased access to news. It would be hard to have secret meetings.

ROBERT: I think it's more than one person. Alexander Hamilton and James Madison probably wrote most of them.

WILLIAM: I'm sure there are other writers as well. I bet John Jay wrote some too.

ROBERT: We also publish the Anti-Federalist Papers. We got an anonymous letter today. The letter was from "Cato." Cato is another Latin name. It means "wise."

WILLIAM: Who do you think Cato is?

ROBERT: It could be George Clinton. Clinton is the governor of New York. But I don't really know.

WILLIAM: What was the letter about?

ROBERT: It warned against strengthening the federal government.

SPOTLIGHT
A SPECIAL EFFECT

We live in a high-tech world. But we are still voting by paper and pen. There are 2 main ways to vote. One, you vote in person. Two, you mail in your vote. Both of these ways require a paper ballot. This means voting by filling in a space. In some cases, machines are used. But today, we do everything on the internet. Some countries use online voting successfully. Why can't we do it in America? There are too many security risks. People don't trust e-voting. They don't believe their vote will be counted. Or they believe hackers will break into online systems. They could change votes. Some states have a form of e-voting. But the e-voting is limited. Our lives have changed since the signing of the Constitution. But we're voting in a similar way.

FLASH FACT!

Federal and state governments handled the COVID-19 pandemic differently. This brought concerns about our system of governing.

WILLIAM: I get it. I worry about giving too much power to a few men. I don't want states to lose power. I worry about having a strong government with a strong president. This could be **tyranny**. We just fought a war. We just freed ourselves from Great Britain.

NARRATOR: *William and Robert are still eating.* **MERCY** *works for William. She comes into the dining area. She serves drinks.*

WILLIAM: What do you think, Mercy?

MERCY: Should I say? No one has asked me about my thoughts.

WILLIAM: Please feel free to share.

MERCY: The Articles of Confederation need to be changed. The states are too loosely connected. They don't work together. How can they protect our country's interests?

ROBERT: How do you know about such things?

MERCY: My father reads the newspaper. He reads out loud every night. I pay attention. It's important to know what's happening.

ROBERT: What do you think about yesterday's news? It talked about **imposing** taxes.

MERCY: Funds are needed to defend our country.

WILLIAM: I don't want to pay taxes.

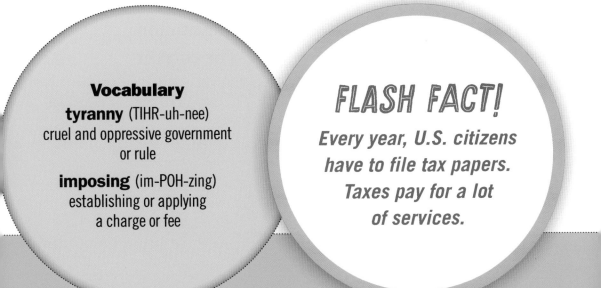

Vocabulary

tyranny (TIHR-uh-nee)
cruel and oppressive government
or rule

imposing (im-POH-zing)
establishing or applying
a charge or fee

FLASH FACT!

Every year, U.S. citizens have to file tax papers. Taxes pay for a lot of services.

MERCY: We need taxes to run our country. Our current government is limited. It doesn't have the power to tax states.

WILLIAM: States are supposed to send money. They're supposed to help.

ROBERT: But they don't do it. That's why we need a stronger national government. A strong government serves the needs of its people.

WILLIAM: We should have the right to **abolish** a government that doesn't serve us.

MERCY: I'm hopeful about this new Constitution. I wouldn't mind a new government. The current government doesn't really serve me.

ROBERT: What do you mean?

MERCY: Only White men with land have rights.
Our government should protect everybody's rights.
Women and people of color should have rights.
We should have a say in how we're governed.

Vocabulary
abolish (uh-BAH-lish)
to end or stop

FLASH FACT!

Women are still fighting for their rights. They want to receive equal pay and to control their own bodies.

ACT 2

NARRATOR: *It is 2022.* **JESSICA, RANDY,** *and* **SALLY** *are students. They go to a school in Philadelphia. Jessica's mom is running for the school board. Jessica, Randy, and Sally are* **volunteers**.

JESSICA: I hope my mom gets elected. She'll be the first Black woman to win.

RANDY: How is that possible? It's 2022.

JESSICA: This area just elects **incumbents**.

SALLY: What does that mean?

JESSICA: The same people win elections. Only White men have held positions.

SALLY: District lines have just changed.

RANDY: Why is that important?

JESSICA: District lines decide where voters vote. Changing these lines changes voters. In our case, this is a good thing. More people of color will be able to vote. My mom will have a winning chance.

Vocabulary

volunteers (vah-luhn-TIHRZ) people who donate their time to help further a cause

incumbents (in-KUHM-buhnts) current holders of an office or position

FLASH FACT!

Activists are working on reforming the districting process.

RANDY: We should change district lines everywhere.

JESSICA: It's not that simple. Changing district lines can be bad. It's used to ensure votes.

Vocabulary

ratified (RA-tuh-fyed) approved or confirmed by voting

restrictions (rih-STRIK-shuhnz) limits or bans

FLASH FACT!

Felons are criminals. They lost the right to vote. Some activists work to reinstate their voting rights.

SALLY: Did you know Patrick Henry tried to change district lines? Henry was against the Constitution. James Madison was for the Constitution. Henry didn't want Madison to win an election. He tried to change district lines.

RANDY: Why did he do that?

SALLY: He wanted to include more voters who were against Madison. His plan didn't work. Madison won. The Constitution was **ratified**.

RANDY: That's a good thing. The Constitution gives people the right to vote.

SALLY: That's not completely true. The Constitution does not state that all citizens have the right to vote. It bans voting **restrictions**.

JESSICA: Also, the Constitution was written in the 1780s. Only White men who owned land were allowed to vote.

SALLY: There's the 15th Amendment. It says voting can't be denied on the basis of race. That happened in 1870.

JESSICA: It only gave voting rights to male citizens. But it denied Native Americans. Native Americans were born here. They couldn't be citizens until 1924. So they couldn't vote.

SALLY: Women couldn't vote until 1920. That's when the 19th Amendment passed. It says voting can't be denied on the basis of sex.

JESSICA: These amendments weren't enough. They didn't protect the right to vote. States are responsible for that. Black people have been denied the right to vote. Many **obstacles** were put in their way.

RANDY: What are some of these obstacles?

JESSICA: For example, there were **poll taxes**. These started in the 1890s. Many Black people were poor. They couldn't pay the poll taxes. This kept them from voting.

U.S. Citizenship
and Immigration
Services

Vocabulary

obstacles (AHB-stuh-kuhlz)
challenges or barriers

poll taxes (POHL TAK-suhz)
voting fees

FLASH FACT!

Immigrants have joined
the military since 1775.
It used to be a way to get
citizenship. But laws
changed. Today, the United
States deports some
of its veterans.

SALLY: There was also a "**grandfather clause**." Some people had **ancestors** who voted before the Civil War. They didn't have to pay poll taxes. This allowed poor White people to vote.

RANDY: Black people weren't able to vote before the Civil War. That clause is unfair. It benefits only White people.

SALLY: The 24th Amendment banned the use of poll taxes in federal elections.

JESSICA: There were other obstacles. For example, some states required voters to pass **literacy** tests. This happened from the 1850s to the 1960s.

RANDY: We have to take tests all the time. That doesn't sound bad.

JESSICA: The literacy tests were a trick. They kept Black people and immigrants from voting. These groups were denied education.

Astronauts have been voting from space since 1997. A Texas law states that voters "who will be on a space flight during the early-voting period and on Election Day, may vote." NASA's Johnson Space Center is in Houston, Texas. Most astronauts live in that city. Dr. Kate Rubins is an astronaut. She has voted from space twice. She voted in the 2016 and 2020 presidential elections. She voted from 200 miles (322 kilometers) out in space. She was orbiting Earth on the International Space Station (ISS). An encrypted electronic ballot is sent to the ISS. Astronauts are emailed a unique passcode. They use this passcode to get their ballots. They cast their votes. They list their address as "low-Earth orbit." They send the ballots to Earth. Official voting workers decode the ballots. They copy the results onto paper ballots and submit them.

Vocabulary

grandfather clause (GRAND-fah-thur KLAWZ) an exemption that allows people to continue with operations that were approved before implementation of a new policy

ancestors (AN-seh-stuhrs) people from whom one is descended

literacy (LIH-tuh-ruh-see) reading and writing skills

FLASH FACT!

People born in the United States and its territories are citizens. But American Samoans are "non-citizen nationals." They can't vote.

RANDY: Our teacher said that **enslaved** people were punished for learning to read.

JESSICA: That's right. They were denied the right to vote for something they weren't allowed to do.

RANDY: It doesn't make any sense. Why would we **suppress** people's voting rights?

SALLY: Voting is power.

JESSICA: It's how we can make changes.

RANDY: The right to vote is our greatest freedom.

JESSICA: We must protect voting rights.

RANDY: We also have to vote.

SALLY: No one is required by law to vote. Voting is a right. It's also a **privilege**.

RANDY: When can we vote?

SALLY: The 26th Amendment addresses this. It says voting can't be denied to citizens who are at least 18 years old.

JESSICA: When I turn 18, I'm voting. That's the first thing I'm doing.

RANDY: I can't wait to vote.

SALLY: Let's change the world.

Vocabulary

enslaved (ihn-SLAYVD)
being forced into slavery

suppress (suh-PRESS)
to stop or put down

privilege (PRIV-lij)
an unearned right or advantage

FLASH FACT!

Some activists want to lower the voting age to 16.

FLASH FORWARD
CURRENT CONNECTIONS

The U.S. Constitution was ratified in 1787. But its legacy lives on. It's a living document. We must protect it. There is still so much work for us to do.

- **Protect voting rights for people with disabilities:** All U.S. citizens have the right to vote. This includes people with disabilities. The Americans with Disabilities Act (ADA) passed in 1990. It protects people with disabilities. People with disabilities may have challenges at polling sites. Some people may need ramps. Some people may need a large-print ballot. Some may need to bring service animals. Polling sites must accommodate special needs. Some sites say it's too expensive to provide these accommodations. It's important to make sure people have access to voting.

- **Fight against voter suppression:** In 2021, Florida passed a restrictive voting law. This law restricts access to mail-in voting. It imposes stricter voter identification requirements. It limits who can pick up and return ballots. It bans private funding for elections. The League of Women Voters of Florida is fighting it. Black Voters Matter is fighting it. Be wary of any laws that limit voting access. It's important to make sure every vote counts.

- **Build trust in our election process:** In 2020, President Donald Trump lost the presidential election. He falsely claimed voter fraud. On January 6, 2021, rioters attacked the U.S. Capitol. The Capitol is the meeting place for Congress. There was a violent riot. These actions created distrust of our election process. It's important to protect our democracy.

CONSIDER THIS!

TAKE A POSITION! Learn more about the Electoral College. There have been at least 700 proposals to change or end it. Many people think we should abolish it. Do you agree or disagree? Argue your point with reasons and evidence.

SAY WHAT? The U.S. Constitution established a national government. It didn't want too much power in one place. Describe the 3 branches of government. Explain how these 3 branches provide checks and balances.

THINK ABOUT IT! In 2020, more than 159 million people voted for president. More votes were cast than in any other U.S. election in history. Why was this the case? How can we continue to increase voter turnout?

Learn More

Baxter, Roberta. *The Creation of the U.S. Constitution.* Ann Arbor, MI: Cherry Lake Publishing, 2015.

Freedman, Russell. *Because They Marched: The People's Campaign for Voting Rights That Changed America.* New York: NY: Holiday House, 2014.

Tyner, Artika R. *Black Voter Suppression: The Fight for the Right to Vote.* Minneapolis, MN: Lerner Publications, 2021.

Winn, Kevin P., and Kelisa Wing. *Voting Rights.* Ann Arbor, MI: Cherry Lake Publishing, 2021.

INDEX

ABOUT THE AUTHOR

Dr. Virginia Loh-Hagan is an author, former K–8 teacher, curriculum designer, and university professor. She's currently the director of the Asian Pacific Islander Desi American (APIDA) Center at San Diego State University. She has voted since she turned 18 years old. She lives in San Diego with her one very tall husband and two very naughty dogs.